BISMILLAAHIR-RAHMAANIR-RAHIIM
In the Name of Allah, Most Gracious, Most Merciful.

All praise and thanks are due to Allah SWT, and
peace and blessings be upon His Messenger SAW.

DAILY
Gratitude
JOURNAL

90-DAY JOURNAL
WITH SECTIONS FOR REFLECTIONS AT TEN DAY INTERVALS

PUBLISHING

Assalaamu 'Alaikum Wa Rahmatullahi Wa Barakatuh.
May Allah's Peace, Mercy and Blessings Be Upon You.

Thank you for choosing this Gratitude Journal.
Strengthen your connection with Allah SWT by reflecting
daily on His Blessings. This 90-Day Journal is designed
to help you start that positive habit.

How to Use This Journal

- Each day, for just a few minutes, write down the things you are grateful for using the 5 prompts provided.
- You can do this in the morning or at the end of the day.
- At every 10-day mark, there is a Reflection page to help you to review your journey at that stage.
- After each Reflection break, continue with your daily gratitude with greater awareness, In Shaa Allah.
- As you progress, we hope that the habit of reflecting upon Allah's bounty becomes part of your daily activities.

May this experience bring you inner peace,
contentment and happiness that is possible only
when we are connected to Allah SWT.
May Allah SWT grant you ease in your journey... Bismillah.

Sincerely,

Aiman Sisters

aiman
PUBLISHING

© Copyright 2021 **AIMAN PUBLISHING**. All rights reserved.

No part of this publication may be reproduced, distributed or transmitted in any form
or by any means, electronic, mechanical, photocopying, recording, or otherwise,
without the prior written permission of the publisher.

Du'ā

"My Lord,
enable me to become grateful
to Your favor that You have
bestowed on me and on my parents,
and to do good deeds that
You like, and admit me,
with Your mercy, among
Your righteous servants."

Al Qur'an 27 : 19

Shukr

DAILY GRATITUDE
DAY 1

DATE: ___ /___ /___

YA ALLAH, PLEASE MAKE TODAY

_____

_____

ALHAMDULILLAH, I'M GRATEFUL FOR

_____

_____

_____

HIGHLIGHTS OF MY DAY

_____

_____

_____

WHAT I LEARNED TODAY

_____

_____

_____

IN SHAA ALLAH, TOMORROW I WILL

Shukr DAILY GRATITUDE
DAY 2

DATE: ___ / ___ / ___

YA ALLAH, PLEASE MAKE TODAY

_____

_____

ALHAMDULILLAH, I'M GRATEFUL FOR

_____

_____

_____

HIGHLIGHTS OF MY DAY

_____

_____

_____

WHAT I LEARNED TODAY

_____

_____

_____

IN SHAA ALLAH, TOMORROW I WILL

Shukr DAILY GRATITUDE
DAY 3

DATE: ___ / ___ / ___

YA ALLAH, PLEASE MAKE TODAY

_____
_____

ALHAMDULILLAH, I'M GRATEFUL FOR

_____
_____
_____

HIGHLIGHTS OF MY DAY

_____
_____
_____

WHAT I LEARNED TODAY

_____
_____
_____

IN SHAA ALLAH, TOMORROW I WILL

Shukr
DAILY GRATITUDE
DAY 4

DATE: ___ /___ /___

YA ALLAH, PLEASE MAKE TODAY

_____

_____

ALHAMDULILLAH, I'M GRATEFUL FOR

_____

_____

_____

HIGHLIGHTS OF MY DAY

_____

_____

_____

WHAT I LEARNED TODAY

_____

_____

_____

IN SHAA ALLAH, TOMORROW I WILL

Shukr DAILY GRATITUDE DAY 5

DATE: ___ /___ /___

YA ALLAH, PLEASE MAKE TODAY

_____

_____

ALHAMDULILLAH, I'M GRATEFUL FOR

_____

_____

_____

HIGHLIGHTS OF MY DAY

_____

_____

_____

WHAT I LEARNED TODAY

_____

_____

_____

IN SHAA ALLAH, TOMORROW I WILL

Shukr DAILY GRATITUDE
DAY 6

DATE: ___ /___ /___

YA ALLAH, PLEASE MAKE TODAY

_____

_____

ALHAMDULILLAH, I'M GRATEFUL FOR

_____

_____

_____

HIGHLIGHTS OF MY DAY

_____

_____

_____

WHAT I LEARNED TODAY

_____

_____

_____

IN SHAA ALLAH, TOMORROW I WILL

Shukr DAILY GRATITUDE DAY 7

DATE: ___ /___ /___

YA ALLAH, PLEASE MAKE TODAY

ALHAMDULILLAH, I'M GRATEFUL FOR

HIGHLIGHTS OF MY DAY

WHAT I LEARNED TODAY

IN SHAA ALLAH, TOMORROW I WILL

Shukr

YA ALLAH, PLEASE MAKE TODAY

_____

_____

ALHAMDULILLAH, I'M GRATEFUL FOR

_____

_____

_____

HIGHLIGHTS OF MY DAY

_____

_____

_____

WHAT I LEARNED TODAY

_____

_____

_____

IN SHAA ALLAH, TOMORROW I WILL

Shukr DAILY GRATITUDE
DAY 9

DATE: ___ / ___ / ___

YA ALLAH, PLEASE MAKE TODAY

ALHAMDULILLAH, I'M GRATEFUL FOR

HIGHLIGHTS OF MY DAY

WHAT I LEARNED TODAY

IN SHAA ALLAH, TOMORROW I WILL

Shukr

DAILY GRATITUDE
DAY 10

DATE: ___ / ___ / ___

YA ALLAH, PLEASE MAKE TODAY

_____

_____

ALHAMDULILLAH, I'M GRATEFUL FOR

_____

_____

_____

HIGHLIGHTS OF MY DAY

_____

_____

_____

WHAT I LEARNED TODAY

_____

_____

_____

IN SHAA ALLAH, TOMORROW I WILL

"And whatever of blessings and good things you have, it is from Allah."

Al Qur'an 16 : 53

Day 10 - REFLECTION

DATE __ / __ / __

ALHAMDULILLAH, MY MOST CHERISHED MOMENTS WERE

_____

_____

_____

_____

_____

I WAS CHALLENGED BY

_____

_____

FROM THESE CHALLENGES, I LEARNED

_____

_____

I SEEK ALLAH'S GUIDANCE FOR

_____

_____

I LOOK FORWARD TO

Shukr DAILY GRATITUDE DAY 11

DATE: ___ / ___ / ___

YA ALLAH, PLEASE MAKE TODAY

_____

_____

ALHAMDULILLAH, I'M GRATEFUL FOR

_____

_____

_____

HIGHLIGHTS OF MY DAY

_____

_____

_____

WHAT I LEARNED TODAY

_____

_____

_____

IN SHAA ALLAH, TOMORROW I WILL

Shukr DAILY GRATITUDE
DAY 12

DATE: ___ / ___ / ___

YA ALLAH, PLEASE MAKE TODAY

ALHAMDULILLAH, I'M GRATEFUL FOR

HIGHLIGHTS OF MY DAY

WHAT I LEARNED TODAY

IN SHAA ALLAH, TOMORROW I WILL

Shukr DAILY GRATITUDE
DAY 13

DATE: ___ / ___ / ___

YA ALLAH, PLEASE MAKE TODAY

_____

_____

ALHAMDULILLAH, I'M GRATEFUL FOR

_____

_____

_____

HIGHLIGHTS OF MY DAY

_____

_____

_____

WHAT I LEARNED TODAY

_____

_____

_____

IN SHAA ALLAH, TOMORROW I WILL

Shukr

DAILY GRATITUDE
DAY 14

DATE: ___ /___ /___

YA ALLAH, PLEASE MAKE TODAY

_____

_____

ALHAMDULILLAH, I'M GRATEFUL FOR

_____

_____

_____

HIGHLIGHTS OF MY DAY

_____

_____

_____

WHAT I LEARNED TODAY

_____

_____

_____

IN SHAA ALLAH, TOMORROW I WILL

Shukr

DAILY GRATITUDE
DAY 15

DATE: ___ /___ /___

YA ALLAH, PLEASE MAKE TODAY

_____

_____

ALHAMDULILLAH, I'M GRATEFUL FOR

_____

_____

_____

HIGHLIGHTS OF MY DAY

_____

_____

_____

WHAT I LEARNED TODAY

_____

_____

_____

IN SHAA ALLAH, TOMORROW I WILL

Shukr DAILY GRATITUDE
DAY 16

DATE: ___ / ___ / ___

YA ALLAH, PLEASE MAKE TODAY

_____

_____

ALHAMDULILLAH, I'M GRATEFUL FOR

_____

_____

_____

HIGHLIGHTS OF MY DAY

_____

_____

_____

WHAT I LEARNED TODAY

_____

_____

_____

IN SHAA ALLAH, TOMORROW I WILL

Shukr DAILY GRATITUDE
DAY 17

DATE: ___ / ___ / ___

YA ALLAH, PLEASE MAKE TODAY

_____

_____

ALHAMDULILLAH, I'M GRATEFUL FOR

_____

_____

_____

HIGHLIGHTS OF MY DAY

_____

_____

_____

WHAT I LEARNED TODAY

_____

_____

_____

IN SHAA ALLAH, TOMORROW I WILL

Shukr DAILY GRATITUDE
DAY 18

DATE: ___ /___ /___

YA ALLAH, PLEASE MAKE TODAY

_____

_____

ALHAMDULILLAH, I'M GRATEFUL FOR

_____

_____

_____

HIGHLIGHTS OF MY DAY

_____

_____

_____

WHAT I LEARNED TODAY

_____

_____

_____

IN SHAA ALLAH, TOMORROW I WILL

Shukr

DAILY GRATITUDE
DAY 19

DATE: ___ /___ /___

YA ALLAH, PLEASE MAKE TODAY

ALHAMDULILLAH, I'M GRATEFUL FOR

HIGHLIGHTS OF MY DAY

WHAT I LEARNED TODAY

IN SHAA ALLAH, TOMORROW I WILL

Shukr DAILY GRATITUDE
DAY 20

DATE: ___ / ___ / ___

YA ALLAH, PLEASE MAKE TODAY

_____

_____

ALHAMDULILLAH, I'M GRATEFUL FOR

_____

_____

_____

HIGHLIGHTS OF MY DAY

_____

_____

_____

WHAT I LEARNED TODAY

_____

_____

_____

IN SHAA ALLAH, TOMORROW I WILL

"Then remember Me;
I will remember you.
Be grateful to Me,
and do not reject Me."

Al Qur'an 2 : 152

Day 20 - REFLECTION   DATE ___/___/___

ALHAMDULILLAH, MY MOST CHERISHED MOMENTS WERE

_____

_____

_____

_____

_____

I WAS CHALLENGED BY

_____

_____

FROM THESE CHALLENGES, I LEARNED

_____

_____

I SEEK ALLAH'S GUIDANCE FOR

_____

_____

I LOOK FORWARD TO

Shukr

DAILY GRATITUDE
DAY 21

DATE: ___ / ___ / ___

YA ALLAH, PLEASE MAKE TODAY

_____

_____

ALHAMDULILLAH, I'M GRATEFUL FOR

_____

_____

_____

HIGHLIGHTS OF MY DAY

_____

_____

_____

WHAT I LEARNED TODAY

_____

_____

_____

IN SHAA ALLAH, TOMORROW I WILL

Shukr DAILY GRATITUDE
DAY 22

DATE: ___ / ___ / ___

YA ALLAH, PLEASE MAKE TODAY

_____

_____

ALHAMDULILLAH, I'M GRATEFUL FOR

_____

_____

_____

HIGHLIGHTS OF MY DAY

_____

_____

_____

WHAT I LEARNED TODAY

_____

_____

_____

IN SHAA ALLAH, TOMORROW I WILL

Shukr DAILY GRATITUDE
DAY 23

DATE: ___ /___ /___

YA ALLAH, PLEASE MAKE TODAY

_____

_____

ALHAMDULILLAH, I'M GRATEFUL FOR

_____

_____

_____

HIGHLIGHTS OF MY DAY

_____

_____

_____

WHAT I LEARNED TODAY

_____

_____

_____

IN SHAA ALLAH, TOMORROW I WILL

Shukr DAILY GRATITUDE
DAY 24

DATE: ___ /___ /___

YA ALLAH, PLEASE MAKE TODAY

_____

_____

ALHAMDULILLAH, I'M GRATEFUL FOR

_____

_____

_____

HIGHLIGHTS OF MY DAY

_____

_____

_____

WHAT I LEARNED TODAY

_____

_____

_____

IN SHAA ALLAH, TOMORROW I WILL

Shukr DAILY GRATITUDE
DAY 25

DATE: ___ /___ /___

YA ALLAH, PLEASE MAKE TODAY

_____
_____

ALHAMDULILLAH, I'M GRATEFUL FOR

_____
_____
_____

HIGHLIGHTS OF MY DAY

_____
_____
_____

WHAT I LEARNED TODAY

_____
_____
_____

IN SHAA ALLAH, TOMORROW I WILL

Shukr

DAILY GRATITUDE
DAY 26

YA ALLAH, PLEASE MAKE TODAY

_____

_____

ALHAMDULILLAH, I'M GRATEFUL FOR

_____

_____

_____

HIGHLIGHTS OF MY DAY

_____

_____

_____

WHAT I LEARNED TODAY

_____

_____

_____

IN SHAA ALLAH, TOMORROW I WILL

Shukr DAILY GRATITUDE DAY 27

DATE: ___ / ___ / ___

YA ALLAH, PLEASE MAKE TODAY

_____

_____

ALHAMDULILLAH, I'M GRATEFUL FOR

_____

_____

_____

HIGHLIGHTS OF MY DAY

_____

_____

_____

WHAT I LEARNED TODAY

_____

_____

_____

IN SHAA ALLAH, TOMORROW I WILL

Shukr

DAILY GRATITUDE
DAY 28

DATE: ___ /___ /___

YA ALLAH, PLEASE MAKE TODAY

_____

_____

ALHAMDULILLAH, I'M GRATEFUL FOR

_____

_____

_____

HIGHLIGHTS OF MY DAY

_____

_____

_____

WHAT I LEARNED TODAY

_____

_____

_____

IN SHAA ALLAH, TOMORROW I WILL

Shukr

DAILY GRATITUDE
DAY 29

DATE: ___ / ___ / ___

YA ALLAH, PLEASE MAKE TODAY

_____

_____

ALHAMDULILLAH, I'M GRATEFUL FOR

_____

_____

_____

HIGHLIGHTS OF MY DAY

_____

_____

WHAT I LEARNED TODAY

_____

_____

IN SHAA ALLAH, TOMORROW I WILL

Shukr DAILY GRATITUDE
DAY 30

DATE: ___ /___ /___

YA ALLAH, PLEASE MAKE TODAY

_____

_____

ALHAMDULILLAH, I'M GRATEFUL FOR

_____

_____

_____

HIGHLIGHTS OF MY DAY

_____

_____

_____

WHAT I LEARNED TODAY

_____

_____

_____

IN SHAA ALLAH, TOMORROW I WILL

"If you are grateful, I would certainly give you more; and if you are ungrateful, My chastisement is truly severe."

Al Qur'an 14 : 7

Day 30 - REFLECTION   DATE __/__/__

ALHAMDULILLAH, MY MOST CHERISHED MOMENTS WERE

_____

_____

_____

_____

_____

I WAS CHALLENGED BY

_____

_____

FROM THESE CHALLENGES, I LEARNED

_____

_____

I SEEK ALLAH'S GUIDANCE FOR

_____

_____

I LOOK FORWARD TO

Shukr

DAILY GRATITUDE
DAY 31

DATE: ___ / ___ / ___

YA ALLAH, PLEASE MAKE TODAY

ALHAMDULILLAH, I'M GRATEFUL FOR

HIGHLIGHTS OF MY DAY

WHAT I LEARNED TODAY

IN SHAA ALLAH, TOMORROW I WILL

Shukr

DAILY GRATITUDE
DAY 32

DATE: ___ / ___ / ___

YA ALLAH, PLEASE MAKE TODAY

_____

_____

ALHAMDULILLAH, I'M GRATEFUL FOR

_____

_____

_____

HIGHLIGHTS OF MY DAY

_____

_____

_____

WHAT I LEARNED TODAY

_____

_____

_____

IN SHAA ALLAH, TOMORROW I WILL

Shukr DAILY GRATITUDE DAY 33

DATE: ___ / ___ / ___

YA ALLAH, PLEASE MAKE TODAY

ALHAMDULILLAH, I'M GRATEFUL FOR

HIGHLIGHTS OF MY DAY

WHAT I LEARNED TODAY

IN SHAA ALLAH, TOMORROW I WILL

Shukr DAILY GRATITUDE
DAY 34

DATE: ___ /___ /___

YA ALLAH, PLEASE MAKE TODAY

_____

_____

ALHAMDULILLAH, I'M GRATEFUL FOR

_____

_____

_____

HIGHLIGHTS OF MY DAY

_____

_____

_____

WHAT I LEARNED TODAY

_____

_____

_____

IN SHAA ALLAH, TOMORROW I WILL

Shukr

DAILY GRATITUDE
DAY 35

DATE: ___ / ___ / ___

YA ALLAH, PLEASE MAKE TODAY

_____

_____

ALHAMDULILLAH, I'M GRATEFUL FOR

_____

_____

_____

HIGHLIGHTS OF MY DAY

_____

_____

_____

WHAT I LEARNED TODAY

_____

_____

_____

IN SHAA ALLAH, TOMORROW I WILL

Shukr DAILY GRATITUDE
DAY 36

DATE: ___ / ___ / ___

YA ALLAH, PLEASE MAKE TODAY

_____

_____

ALHAMDULILLAH, I'M GRATEFUL FOR

_____

_____

_____

HIGHLIGHTS OF MY DAY

_____

_____

_____

WHAT I LEARNED TODAY

_____

_____

_____

IN SHAA ALLAH, TOMORROW I WILL

Shukr

DAILY GRATITUDE
DAY 37

DATE: ___ / ___ / ___

YA ALLAH, PLEASE MAKE TODAY

ALHAMDULILLAH, I'M GRATEFUL FOR

HIGHLIGHTS OF MY DAY

WHAT I LEARNED TODAY

IN SHAA ALLAH, TOMORROW I WILL

Shukr

DAILY GRATITUDE
DAY 38

DATE: ___ / ___ / ___

YA ALLAH, PLEASE MAKE TODAY

_____

_____

ALHAMDULILLAH, I'M GRATEFUL FOR

_____

_____

_____

HIGHLIGHTS OF MY DAY

_____

_____

_____

WHAT I LEARNED TODAY

_____

_____

_____

IN SHAA ALLAH, TOMORROW I WILL

Shukr

DAILY GRATITUDE
DAY 39

DATE: ___ / ___ / ___

YA ALLAH, PLEASE MAKE TODAY

_____

_____

ALHAMDULILLAH, I'M GRATEFUL FOR

_____

_____

_____

HIGHLIGHTS OF MY DAY

_____

_____

_____

WHAT I LEARNED TODAY

_____

_____

_____

IN SHAA ALLAH, TOMORROW I WILL

Shukr DAILY GRATITUDE
DAY 40

DATE: ___ / ___ / ___

YA ALLAH, PLEASE MAKE TODAY

_____

_____

ALHAMDULILLAH, I'M GRATEFUL FOR

_____

_____

_____

HIGHLIGHTS OF MY DAY

_____

_____

_____

WHAT I LEARNED TODAY

_____

_____

_____

IN SHAA ALLAH, TOMORROW I WILL

"...Anyone who is grateful does so to the profit of his own soul..."

Al Qur'an 31 : 12

Day 40 - REFLECTION   DATE __ / __ / __

ALHAMDULILLAH, MY MOST CHERISHED MOMENTS WERE

_____

_____

_____

_____

_____

I WAS CHALLENGED BY

_____

_____

FROM THESE CHALLENGES, I LEARNED

_____

_____

I SEEK ALLAH'S GUIDANCE FOR

_____

_____

I LOOK FORWARD TO

Shukr

DAILY GRATITUDE
DAY 41

DATE: ___ / ___ / ___

YA ALLAH, PLEASE MAKE TODAY

_____

_____

ALHAMDULILLAH, I'M GRATEFUL FOR

_____

_____

_____

HIGHLIGHTS OF MY DAY

_____

_____

_____

WHAT I LEARNED TODAY

_____

_____

_____

IN SHAA ALLAH, TOMORROW I WILL

Shukr

YA ALLAH, PLEASE MAKE TODAY

_____

_____

ALHAMDULILLAH, I'M GRATEFUL FOR

_____

_____

_____

HIGHLIGHTS OF MY DAY

_____

_____

_____

WHAT I LEARNED TODAY

_____

_____

_____

IN SHAA ALLAH, TOMORROW I WILL

Shukr

DAILY GRATITUDE
DAY 43

DATE: ___ /___ /___

YA ALLAH, PLEASE MAKE TODAY

_____

_____

ALHAMDULILLAH, I'M GRATEFUL FOR

_____

_____

_____

HIGHLIGHTS OF MY DAY

_____

_____

_____

WHAT I LEARNED TODAY

_____

_____

_____

IN SHAA ALLAH, TOMORROW I WILL

Shukr

DAILY GRATITUDE
DAY 44

DATE: ___ /___ /___

YA ALLAH, PLEASE MAKE TODAY

_____

_____

ALHAMDULILLAH, I'M GRATEFUL FOR

_____

_____

_____

HIGHLIGHTS OF MY DAY

_____

_____

_____

WHAT I LEARNED TODAY

_____

_____

_____

IN SHAA ALLAH, TOMORROW I WILL

Shukr DAILY GRATITUDE
DAY 45

DATE: ___ /___ /___

YA ALLAH, PLEASE MAKE TODAY

_____

_____

ALHAMDULILLAH, I'M GRATEFUL FOR

_____

_____

_____

HIGHLIGHTS OF MY DAY

_____

_____

_____

WHAT I LEARNED TODAY

_____

_____

_____

IN SHAA ALLAH, TOMORROW I WILL

Shukr DAILY GRATITUDE
DAY 46

DATE: ___ /___ /___

YA ALLAH, PLEASE MAKE TODAY

_____

_____

ALHAMDULILLAH, I'M GRATEFUL FOR

_____

_____

_____

HIGHLIGHTS OF MY DAY

_____

_____

_____

WHAT I LEARNED TODAY

_____

_____

_____

IN SHAA ALLAH, TOMORROW I WILL

Shukr

DAILY GRATITUDE
DAY 47

DATE: ___ / ___ / ___

YA ALLAH, PLEASE MAKE TODAY

_____

_____

ALHAMDULILLAH, I'M GRATEFUL FOR

_____

_____

_____

HIGHLIGHTS OF MY DAY

_____

_____

_____

WHAT I LEARNED TODAY

_____

_____

_____

IN SHAA ALLAH, TOMORROW I WILL

Shukr

DAILY GRATITUDE
DAY 48

DATE: ___ / ___ / ___

YA ALLAH, PLEASE MAKE TODAY

_____

_____

ALHAMDULILLAH, I'M GRATEFUL FOR

_____

_____

_____

HIGHLIGHTS OF MY DAY

_____

_____

_____

WHAT I LEARNED TODAY

_____

_____

_____

IN SHAA ALLAH, TOMORROW I WILL

Shukr
DAILY GRATITUDE
DAY 49

DATE: ___ / ___ / ___

YA ALLAH, PLEASE MAKE TODAY

_____

_____

ALHAMDULILLAH, I'M GRATEFUL FOR

_____

_____

_____

HIGHLIGHTS OF MY DAY

_____

_____

_____

WHAT I LEARNED TODAY

_____

_____

_____

IN SHAA ALLAH, TOMORROW I WILL

Shukr DAILY GRATITUDE
DAY 50

DATE: ___ /___ /___

YA ALLAH, PLEASE MAKE TODAY

_____
_____

ALHAMDULILLAH, I'M GRATEFUL FOR

_____
_____
_____

HIGHLIGHTS OF MY DAY

_____
_____
_____

WHAT I LEARNED TODAY

_____
_____
_____

IN SHAA ALLAH, TOMORROW I WILL

"...and Allah will give reward to those who are grateful."

Al Qur'an 3 : 144

Day 50 - REFLECTION

DATE __ / __ / __

ALHAMDULILLAH, MY MOST CHERISHED MOMENTS WERE

_____

_____

_____

_____

_____

I WAS CHALLENGED BY

_____

_____

FROM THESE CHALLENGES, I LEARNED

_____

_____

I SEEK ALLAH'S GUIDANCE FOR

_____

_____

I LOOK FORWARD TO

Shukr

DAILY GRATITUDE
DAY 51

DATE: ___ / ___ / ___

YA ALLAH, PLEASE MAKE TODAY

_____

_____

ALHAMDULILLAH, I'M GRATEFUL FOR

_____

_____

_____

HIGHLIGHTS OF MY DAY

_____

_____

_____

WHAT I LEARNED TODAY

_____

_____

_____

IN SHAA ALLAH, TOMORROW I WILL

Shukr DAILY GRATITUDE
DAY 52

DATE: ___ /___ /___

YA ALLAH, PLEASE MAKE TODAY

_____

_____

ALHAMDULILLAH, I'M GRATEFUL FOR

_____

_____

_____

HIGHLIGHTS OF MY DAY

_____

_____

_____

WHAT I LEARNED TODAY

_____

_____

_____

IN SHAA ALLAH, TOMORROW I WILL

Shukr DAILY GRATITUDE
DAY 53

DATE: ___ /___ /___

YA ALLAH, PLEASE MAKE TODAY

_____

_____

_____

ALHAMDULILLAH, I'M GRATEFUL FOR

_____

_____

_____

_____

HIGHLIGHTS OF MY DAY

_____

_____

_____

_____

WHAT I LEARNED TODAY

_____

_____

_____

IN SHAA ALLAH, TOMORROW I WILL

Shukr DAILY GRATITUDE
DAY 54

DATE: ___ / ___ / ___

YA ALLAH, PLEASE MAKE TODAY

_____

_____

ALHAMDULILLAH, I'M GRATEFUL FOR

_____

_____

_____

HIGHLIGHTS OF MY DAY

_____

_____

_____

WHAT I LEARNED TODAY

_____

_____

_____

IN SHAA ALLAH, TOMORROW I WILL

Shukr
DAILY GRATITUDE
DAY 55

DATE: ___ / ___ / ___

YA ALLAH, PLEASE MAKE TODAY

_____

_____

ALHAMDULILLAH, I'M GRATEFUL FOR

_____

_____

_____

HIGHLIGHTS OF MY DAY

_____

_____

_____

WHAT I LEARNED TODAY

_____

_____

_____

IN SHAA ALLAH, TOMORROW I WILL

Shukr DAILY GRATITUDE
DAY 56

DATE: ___ / ___ / ___

YA ALLAH, PLEASE MAKE TODAY

_____

_____

ALHAMDULILLAH, I'M GRATEFUL FOR

_____

_____

_____

HIGHLIGHTS OF MY DAY

_____

_____

_____

WHAT I LEARNED TODAY

_____

_____

_____

IN SHAA ALLAH, TOMORROW I WILL

Shukr DAILY GRATITUDE
DAY 57

DATE: ___ / ___ / ___

YA ALLAH, PLEASE MAKE TODAY

_____

_____

ALHAMDULILLAH, I'M GRATEFUL FOR

_____

_____

_____

HIGHLIGHTS OF MY DAY

_____

_____

_____

WHAT I LEARNED TODAY

_____

_____

_____

IN SHAA ALLAH, TOMORROW I WILL

Shukr DAILY GRATITUDE
DAY 58

DATE: ___ / ___ / ___

YA ALLAH, PLEASE MAKE TODAY

_____

_____

ALHAMDULILLAH, I'M GRATEFUL FOR

_____

_____

_____

HIGHLIGHTS OF MY DAY

_____

_____

_____

WHAT I LEARNED TODAY

_____

_____

_____

IN SHAA ALLAH, TOMORROW I WILL

Shukr
DAILY GRATITUDE
DAY 59

DATE: ___ /___ /___

YA ALLAH, PLEASE MAKE TODAY

_____

_____

ALHAMDULILLAH, I'M GRATEFUL FOR

_____

_____

_____

HIGHLIGHTS OF MY DAY

_____

_____

_____

WHAT I LEARNED TODAY

_____

_____

_____

IN SHAA ALLAH, TOMORROW I WILL

Shukr

DAILY GRATITUDE
DAY 60

DATE: ___ / ___ / ___

YA ALLAH, PLEASE MAKE TODAY

_____

_____

ALHAMDULILLAH, I'M GRATEFUL FOR

_____

_____

_____

HIGHLIGHTS OF MY DAY

_____

_____

_____

WHAT I LEARNED TODAY

_____

_____

_____

IN SHAA ALLAH, TOMORROW I WILL

"...If anyone desires a
reward in this life,
We shall give it to him;
and if anyone desires
a reward in the Hereafter,
We shall give it to him.
And swiftly shall We
reward those that
(serve us with) gratitude."

Al Qur'an 3 : 145

Day 60 - REFLECTION

DATE __ / __ / __

ALHAMDULILLAH, MY MOST CHERISHED MOMENTS WERE

_____

_____

_____

_____

_____

I WAS CHALLENGED BY

_____

_____

FROM THESE CHALLENGES, I LEARNED

_____

_____

I SEEK ALLAH'S GUIDANCE FOR

_____

_____

I LOOK FORWARD TO

Shukr DAILY GRATITUDE
DAY 61

DATE: ___ / ___ / ___

YA ALLAH, PLEASE MAKE TODAY

_____

_____

ALHAMDULILLAH, I'M GRATEFUL FOR

_____

_____

_____

HIGHLIGHTS OF MY DAY

_____

_____

_____

WHAT I LEARNED TODAY

_____

_____

_____

IN SHAA ALLAH, TOMORROW I WILL

Shukr
DAILY GRATITUDE
DAY 62

DATE: ___ / ___ / ___

YA ALLAH, PLEASE MAKE TODAY

_____

_____

ALHAMDULILLAH, I'M GRATEFUL FOR

_____

_____

_____

HIGHLIGHTS OF MY DAY

_____

_____

_____

WHAT I LEARNED TODAY

_____

_____

_____

IN SHAA ALLAH, TOMORROW I WILL

Shukr DAILY GRATITUDE
DAY 63

DATE: ___ / ___ / ___

YA ALLAH, PLEASE MAKE TODAY

ALHAMDULILLAH, I'M GRATEFUL FOR

HIGHLIGHTS OF MY DAY

WHAT I LEARNED TODAY

IN SHAA ALLAH, TOMORROW I WILL

Shukr DAILY GRATITUDE
DAY 64

DATE: ___ / ___ / ___

YA ALLAH, PLEASE MAKE TODAY

_____

_____

ALHAMDULILLAH, I'M GRATEFUL FOR

_____

_____

_____

HIGHLIGHTS OF MY DAY

_____

_____

_____

WHAT I LEARNED TODAY

_____

_____

_____

IN SHAA ALLAH, TOMORROW I WILL

Shukr DAILY GRATITUDE
DAY 65

DATE: ___ /___ /___

YA ALLAH, PLEASE MAKE TODAY

ALHAMDULILLAH, I'M GRATEFUL FOR

HIGHLIGHTS OF MY DAY

WHAT I LEARNED TODAY

IN SHAA ALLAH, TOMORROW I WILL

Shukr DAILY GRATITUDE
DAY 66

DATE: ___ / ___ / ___

YA ALLAH, PLEASE MAKE TODAY

_____

_____

ALHAMDULILLAH, I'M GRATEFUL FOR

_____

_____

_____

HIGHLIGHTS OF MY DAY

_____

_____

_____

WHAT I LEARNED TODAY

_____

_____

_____

IN SHAA ALLAH, TOMORROW I WILL

Shukr
DAILY GRATITUDE
DAY 67

DATE: ___ / ___ / ___

YA ALLAH, PLEASE MAKE TODAY

ALHAMDULILLAH, I'M GRATEFUL FOR

HIGHLIGHTS OF MY DAY

WHAT I LEARNED TODAY

IN SHAA ALLAH, TOMORROW I WILL

Shukr

DAILY GRATITUDE
DAY 68

DATE: ___ / ___ / ___

YA ALLAH, PLEASE MAKE TODAY

_____

_____

ALHAMDULILLAH, I'M GRATEFUL FOR

_____

_____

_____

HIGHLIGHTS OF MY DAY

_____

_____

_____

WHAT I LEARNED TODAY

_____

_____

_____

IN SHAA ALLAH, TOMORROW I WILL

Shukr DAILY GRATITUDE DAY 69

DATE: ___ /___ /___

YA ALLAH, PLEASE MAKE TODAY

ALHAMDULILLAH, I'M GRATEFUL FOR

HIGHLIGHTS OF MY DAY

WHAT I LEARNED TODAY

IN SHAA ALLAH, TOMORROW I WILL

Shukr DAILY GRATITUDE
DAY 70

DATE: ___ / ___ / ___

YA ALLAH, PLEASE MAKE TODAY

_____

_____

ALHAMDULILLAH, I'M GRATEFUL FOR

_____

_____

_____

HIGHLIGHTS OF MY DAY

_____

_____

_____

WHAT I LEARNED TODAY

_____

_____

_____

IN SHAA ALLAH, TOMORROW I WILL

"And whoever puts all
his trust in Allah,
He will be enough
for him. "

Al Qur'an 65 : 3

Day 70 - REFLECTION

DATE ___ / ___ / ___

ALHAMDULILLAH, MY MOST CHERISHED MOMENTS WERE

I WAS CHALLENGED BY

FROM THESE CHALLENGES, I LEARNED

I SEEK ALLAH'S GUIDANCE FOR

I LOOK FORWARD TO

Shukr

DAILY GRATITUDE
DAY 71

DATE: ___ / ___ / ___

YA ALLAH, PLEASE MAKE TODAY

_____

_____

ALHAMDULILLAH, I'M GRATEFUL FOR

_____

_____

_____

HIGHLIGHTS OF MY DAY

_____

_____

_____

WHAT I LEARNED TODAY

_____

_____

_____

IN SHAA ALLAH, TOMORROW I WILL

Shukr

DAILY GRATITUDE
DAY 72

DATE: ___ / ___ / ___

YA ALLAH, PLEASE MAKE TODAY

_____

_____

ALHAMDULILLAH, I'M GRATEFUL FOR

_____

_____

_____

HIGHLIGHTS OF MY DAY

_____

_____

_____

WHAT I LEARNED TODAY

_____

_____

_____

IN SHAA ALLAH, TOMORROW I WILL

Shukr

DAILY GRATITUDE
DAY 73

DATE: ___ /___ /___

YA ALLAH, PLEASE MAKE TODAY

ALHAMDULILLAH, I'M GRATEFUL FOR

HIGHLIGHTS OF MY DAY

WHAT I LEARNED TODAY

IN SHAA ALLAH, TOMORROW I WILL

Shukr DAILY GRATITUDE
DAY 74

DATE: ___ /___ /___

YA ALLAH, PLEASE MAKE TODAY

_____

_____

ALHAMDULILLAH, I'M GRATEFUL FOR

_____

_____

_____

HIGHLIGHTS OF MY DAY

_____

_____

_____

WHAT I LEARNED TODAY

_____

_____

_____

IN SHAA ALLAH, TOMORROW I WILL

Shukr

DAILY GRATITUDE
DAY 75

DATE: ___ /___ /___

YA ALLAH, PLEASE MAKE TODAY

_____

_____

ALHAMDULILLAH, I'M GRATEFUL FOR

_____

_____

_____

HIGHLIGHTS OF MY DAY

_____

_____

_____

WHAT I LEARNED TODAY

_____

_____

_____

IN SHAA ALLAH, TOMORROW I WILL

Shukr DAILY GRATITUDE
DAY 76

DATE: ___ / ___ / ___

YA ALLAH, PLEASE MAKE TODAY

_____

_____

ALHAMDULILLAH, I'M GRATEFUL FOR

_____

_____

_____

HIGHLIGHTS OF MY DAY

_____

_____

_____

WHAT I LEARNED TODAY

_____

_____

_____

IN SHAA ALLAH, TOMORROW I WILL

Shukr

DAILY GRATITUDE
DAY 77

DATE: ___ / ___ / ___

YA ALLAH, PLEASE MAKE TODAY

_____

_____

ALHAMDULILLAH, I'M GRATEFUL FOR

_____

_____

_____

HIGHLIGHTS OF MY DAY

_____

_____

_____

WHAT I LEARNED TODAY

_____

_____

_____

IN SHAA ALLAH, TOMORROW I WILL

Shukr DAILY GRATITUDE
DAY 78

DATE: ___ / ___ / ___

YA ALLAH, PLEASE MAKE TODAY

_____

_____

ALHAMDULILLAH, I'M GRATEFUL FOR

_____

_____

_____

HIGHLIGHTS OF MY DAY

_____

_____

_____

WHAT I LEARNED TODAY

_____

_____

_____

IN SHAA ALLAH, TOMORROW I WILL

Shukr DAILY GRATITUDE
DAY 79

DATE: ___ /___ /___

YA ALLAH, PLEASE MAKE TODAY

_____

_____

ALHAMDULILLAH, I'M GRATEFUL FOR

_____

_____

_____

HIGHLIGHTS OF MY DAY

_____

_____

_____

WHAT I LEARNED TODAY

_____

_____

_____

IN SHAA ALLAH, TOMORROW I WILL

Shukr DAILY GRATITUDE DAY 80

DATE: ___ / ___ / ___

YA ALLAH, PLEASE MAKE TODAY

_____

_____

ALHAMDULILLAH, I'M GRATEFUL FOR

_____

_____

_____

HIGHLIGHTS OF MY DAY

_____

_____

_____

WHAT I LEARNED TODAY

_____

_____

_____

IN SHAA ALLAH, TOMORROW I WILL

"Then eat of what Allah
has provided for you
(which is) lawful and good.
And be grateful for
the favor of Allah,
if it is (indeed) Him
that you worship."

Al Qur'an 16 : 114

Day 80 - REFLECTION

DATE __ / __ / __

ALHAMDULILLAH, MY MOST CHERISHED MOMENTS WERE

_____

_____

_____

_____

_____

I WAS CHALLENGED BY

_____

_____

FROM THESE CHALLENGES, I LEARNED

_____

_____

I SEEK ALLAH'S GUIDANCE FOR

_____

_____

I LOOK FORWARD TO

Shukr

DAILY GRATITUDE
DAY 81

DATE: ___ / ___ / ___

YA ALLAH, PLEASE MAKE TODAY

ALHAMDULILLAH, I'M GRATEFUL FOR

HIGHLIGHTS OF MY DAY

WHAT I LEARNED TODAY

IN SHAA ALLAH, TOMORROW I WILL

Shukr DAILY GRATITUDE DAY 82

DATE: ___ /___ /___

YA ALLAH, PLEASE MAKE TODAY

ALHAMDULILLAH, I'M GRATEFUL FOR

HIGHLIGHTS OF MY DAY

WHAT I LEARNED TODAY

IN SHAA ALLAH, TOMORROW I WILL

Shukr DAILY GRATITUDE DAY 83

DATE: ___ / ___ / ___

YA ALLAH, PLEASE MAKE TODAY

ALHAMDULILLAH, I'M GRATEFUL FOR

HIGHLIGHTS OF MY DAY

WHAT I LEARNED TODAY

IN SHAA ALLAH, TOMORROW I WILL

Shukr
DAILY GRATITUDE
DAY 84

DATE: ___ / ___ / ___

YA ALLAH, PLEASE MAKE TODAY

_____

_____

ALHAMDULILLAH, I'M GRATEFUL FOR

_____

_____

_____

HIGHLIGHTS OF MY DAY

_____

_____

_____

WHAT I LEARNED TODAY

_____

_____

_____

IN SHAA ALLAH, TOMORROW I WILL

Shukr DAILY GRATITUDE
DAY 85

DATE: ___ / ___ / ___

YA ALLAH, PLEASE MAKE TODAY

_____

_____

ALHAMDULILLAH, I'M GRATEFUL FOR

_____

_____

_____

HIGHLIGHTS OF MY DAY

_____

_____

_____

WHAT I LEARNED TODAY

_____

_____

_____

IN SHAA ALLAH, TOMORROW I WILL

Shukr DAILY GRATITUDE
DAY 86

YA ALLAH, PLEASE MAKE TODAY

_____

_____

ALHAMDULILLAH, I'M GRATEFUL FOR

_____

_____

_____

HIGHLIGHTS OF MY DAY

_____

_____

_____

WHAT I LEARNED TODAY

_____

_____

_____

IN SHAA ALLAH, TOMORROW I WILL

Shukr DAILY GRATITUDE
DAY 87

DATE: ___ / ___ / ___

YA ALLAH, PLEASE MAKE TODAY

ALHAMDULILLAH, I'M GRATEFUL FOR

HIGHLIGHTS OF MY DAY

WHAT I LEARNED TODAY

IN SHAA ALLAH, TOMORROW I WILL

Shukr DAILY GRATITUDE
DAY 88

DATE: ___ / ___ / ___

YA ALLAH, PLEASE MAKE TODAY

_____

_____

ALHAMDULILLAH, I'M GRATEFUL FOR

_____

_____

_____

HIGHLIGHTS OF MY DAY

_____

_____

_____

WHAT I LEARNED TODAY

_____

_____

_____

IN SHAA ALLAH, TOMORROW I WILL

Shukr
DAILY GRATITUDE
DAY 89

DATE: ___ /___ /___

YA ALLAH, PLEASE MAKE TODAY

_____

_____

ALHAMDULILLAH, I'M GRATEFUL FOR

_____

_____

_____

HIGHLIGHTS OF MY DAY

_____

_____

_____

WHAT I LEARNED TODAY

_____

_____

_____

IN SHAA ALLAH, TOMORROW I WILL

Shukr DAILY GRATITUDE
DAY 90

DATE: ___ /___ /___

YA ALLAH, PLEASE MAKE TODAY

_____

_____

ALHAMDULILLAH, I'M GRATEFUL FOR

_____

_____

_____

HIGHLIGHTS OF MY DAY

_____

_____

_____

WHAT I LEARNED TODAY

_____

_____

_____

IN SHAA ALLAH, TOMORROW I WILL

"...my success comes only through Allah. In Him I trust and to Him I turn."

Al Qur'an 11 : 88

Day 90 - REFLECTION   DATE __ / __ / __

ALHAMDULILLAH, MY MOST CHERISHED MOMENTS WERE

_____

_____

_____

_____

_____

I WAS CHALLENGED BY

_____

_____

FROM THESE CHALLENGES, I LEARNED

_____

_____

I SEEK ALLAH'S GUIDANCE FOR

_____

_____

I LOOK FORWARD TO

Alhamdulillah, we have come to
end of this 90-Day Gratitude Journal.
We hope that you've had a fulfilling journey in
the path towards Allah SWT.

May Allah SWT accept your good deeds,
open more doors of goodness and shower His
Blessings on you and your loved ones.

Sincerely.

Aiman Sisters

P/S - If you wish order another copy of this journal
or wish to check out our other
Islamic journals and notebooks, please visit
www.amazon.com/author/aimanpublishing.

MADE WITH LOVE BY

aiman
PUBLISHING

Notes

Notes

Notes

Notes

Notes

Notes

Notes

Notes